Learn Acoustic Guitar, Classic Fingerstyle

CW00952070

Favorite Greek Songs

Dr Alex Davidovic   Professor Milan Mitic

Contents

Introduction

Why are there so many people who learn to play a little but never become very good at it?

Traditionally, learning to read the sheet music is hard, and I am yet to find a child or an adult who loves to practice scales for hours. Alas, perfecting your technique takes lots of practice.

To speed up your learning to the point when you can easily play complex melodies quickly, this book is more than just a book. It is an entire course comprising music scores, audio files, and videos. What binds it together is the FAME (Fast Acoustic-guitar Mastery by Example) method for the rapid guitar mastery, which Professor Milan Mitic and I have developed. For us, writing this book was the labor of love, with my work focused on the guitar pieces selection and editing, and Milan doing all the arrangements.

The FAME method works in classroom situations with a teacher, or in one-on-one training with an instructor, or when you wish to learn on your own. In any case, it makes it possible to play the great tunes that students typically learn after 2 or 3 years of music school in a matter of weeks. It truly is the closest you'll ever come to a 'magic bullet'.

By adding your personal touch, you'll be developing your own unique playing style from the start.

FAME is a simple, straightforward and highly efficient 4-step method:

1. Listen
Listen to the audio recording and imagine playing it.

2. Watch
Watch the video while skimming over the sheet music, the left hand and the right hand technique.

3. Do
Watch the step-by-step slow-motion part of the video with the sheet music in front of you, and learn the whole song, bit by bit, and

4. Repeat
Practice until it's perfect!

Step 1 : Listen and Visualize

Close your eyes, listen to the audio recording and in your mind make a picture of you playing it. Listen to the recording 3 times, each time adding more detail until you have the perfect picture. Some people imagine being in front of cameras with millions of people from all over the world listening to them. Others think of being with their friends… or their loved one. There is no right and wrong here, but the important thingi s that this internal picture needs to be perfect FOR YOU.

It's a simple step, but an essential one-do not try to make a shortcut and skip it. In this step you are using the power of positive visualization.

In one experiment, the students who have never played tennis before were divided into two groups. One group received the introductory tennis lesson. The other group were shown the images of hitting the forehand and the backhand and told how to imagine doing the perfect shot. After that, the two groups were tested - and the second group, the one using positive imagination, performed considerably better than the first one. Why is that? Because this mental rehearsal does 3 things:

- It builds your motivation and mobilizes your internal forces
- It primes your brain with the task at hand, and
- It activates your subconscious creativity.

Positive visualization is used by top performers and professional athletes. It also works for musicians. To make the most of it, in your mind involve as many senses as you can. The music is what you are actually hearing - and to make this experience as valuable as possible, we only use the studio recordings in our FAME-based tutoring programs. We have to invest a lot more time to do it and it brings up our production costs, but for you it means the much better experience and the much better results. So, the music is what you are actually hearing, and the rest is constructed internally. In your mind, see the scene around you as you perform the piece. How would this look like? What would it smell like? How would your fingertips feel as you play the tune?

I'd like to stress one thing out: positive visualization is not the replacement for the actual practice as some so-called "gurus" would like you to believe. There is no such thing as the "law-of-attraction" - no-one has become rich,or a top athlete, or a great musician solely by imagining it. The power of positive visualization is a great thing, though, because it prepares you for the other 3 steps, and maximizes them in the best possible manner.

Step2: Watch

In this step you watch the video 3 times with the sheet music in front of you. Every FAME course has 2-part videos: the first part showing exactly how the piece is performed, and what the left and the right hands are doing, and the second part showing everything bit-by-bit, in slow motion. So, in the first step you listen, and in the second step you connect what you're hearing to the sheet music, picking and fingering. You watch the video 3 times:

- The first time you watch the video while skimming over the sheet music in front of you
- The second time you focus on what the left hand is doing, and
- The third time you watch the video, you focus on what the right hand is doing.

To recap, the second step helps you connect the dots, so to speak. At this stage you do not even have your guitar with you. Instead, you see how the piece is being performed while focusing on the notes, the left hand and the right hand. This all helps create the right pathways in your brain in preparation for the third step.

Step 3: Do

In this step, you work mostly with the second part of the video, the one showing everything bit-by-bit and in slow motion. Watch this part of the video with the sheet music in front of you, and learn the whole piece, bit by bit.

Every time you learn a section, go to the first part of the video, the one showing how the entire piece is performed, and compare it to what you've been doing. The Latin principle of "Divide et impera", or in English 'Divide and conquer" does not apply only to economics, politics orsociology, it also applies to music.

Every piece of music, no matter how hard or complex it may appear at first, can be mastered using this technique: by dividing it in to segments and learning them one by one. You learn one bit, then another bit, then you put them together -and in no time you learn the lot and are able to perform the entire piece.

The first 3 steps would not be complete without the fourth one. As the old Latins would put it, "Repetitio est mater studiorum" , or in English, "The repetition is the mother of learning". You've probably guessed it, the fourth and final step is:

Step 4: Repeat

Practice until it's perfect! The end result is the guitar mastery at your fingertips. Please note: follow these 4 steps in order, do not try to cheat, and you'll be amazed with the results. It is the simplest, most effective way to master the guitar available today.

A Fishing Boat

Boat from Chios

2

Irene

O Haralambis

Pera Stous

Samiotissa

2

Strose To Stroma

Tsakonian Dance

pizz.....................

Ikariotikos

Gerakina

Karaguna

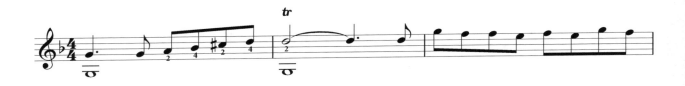

2

3

Sikon (Opa Ni Na Nai)

Miserlou

D. C al Fine

Tin Agapi Mu

Trava Trava

35

Yerakina

Make sure to check out our other book **"Learn Acoustic Guitar Classic Fingerstyle: Beginner's Course"**, at **FAMEguitar.com**

When it comes to learning to play the guitar, getting started is usually the hardest part. This book makes it as easy as humanly possible, via FAME (Fast Acoustic-guitar Mastery by Example) method which combines music scores, audio and video to help you start playing great tunes quickly.

By the time you finish the book, you'll be able to read the sheet music, hold the guitar properly, apply the picking and strumming techniques, and play **Malaguena** and other beautiful tunes that everyone loves to hear:

Malaguena

Check out our other book **"Learn Acoustic Guitar, Classic Fingerstyle: Nursery Rhymes and Christmas Carols"**, which is available at **FAMEguitar.com**. Learn to play **'We Wish You a Merry Christmas'** and 45 other beautiful tunes.

We Wish You a Merry Christmas

Take a look at another book in the series, **"Learn Acoustic Guitar, Classic Finger-style: Christmas Carols Volume 2"**, at **FAMEguitar.com**. Learn to play **'A La Nanita Nana'** and a lot more.

A La Nanita Nana

Los Peces en el Rio

New to playing guitar, or want to brush up your skills? Get **"Learn Acoustic Guitar, Classic Fingerstyle: Traditional English Songs"**, which is available at **FAMEguitar.com**, and in no time you'll be playing the tunes like the one below:

For He's a Jolly Good Fellow

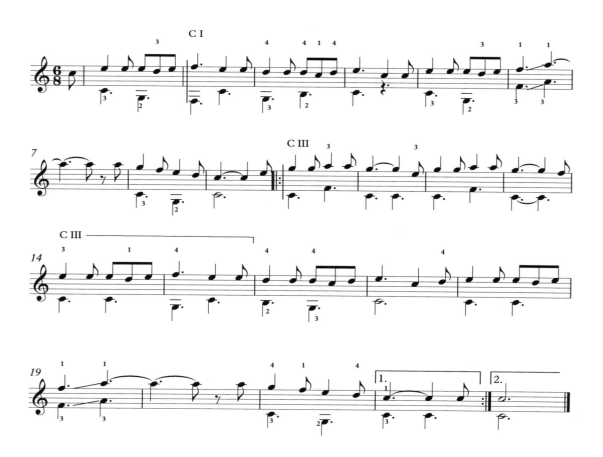

Your Next Step

Always go back to the basics! If you'd like to speed up your progress and make sure that you are doing everything the right way, sign up for online coaching via Skype at FAMEGuitar.com/coaching. Remember, it is many TIMES easier to learn everything the right way when you're building the foundations, then to undo the bad habits later.

Getting the Audios and Videos

All the audios are studio recordings, and all the videos are High Definition. They are supplied online as an integral part of this book.

To access all the audios and videos, please go to:
http://FAMEGuitar.com/videos

For more FAME-based guitar books and courses, and to join the community of people who love the acoustic guitar, visit us at:
http://FAMEGuitar.com

We cannot wait to see you perform!

Dr Alex Davidovic
Professor Milan Mitic